I0221908

Anthony Trollope

How the Mastiffs Went to Iceland

Anthony Trollope

How the Mastiffs Went to Iceland

ISBN/EAN: 9783337316365

Printed in Europe, USA, Canada, Australia, Japan

Cover: Foto ©ninafisch / pixelio.de

More available books at **www.hansebooks.com**

HOW THE "MASTIFFS" WENT TO ICELAND

By ANTHONY TROLLOPE

WITH ILLUSTRATIONS BY MRS. HUGH BLACKBURN

LIST OF ILLUSTRATIONS.

HOW THE "MASTIFFS" WENT TO ICELAND.

CHAPTER I.

THE following few pages are a record,—as are the accompanying illustrations a much better record,—of the trip we took to Iceland in June and July, 1878. The trip was taken in the *Mastiff*, and "we" among ourselves were known only as the "Mastiffs." The "Mastiffs" were as follows:

Mr. JOHN BURNS	. *Our Host.*
Mrs. JOHN BURNS	. *Our Hostess.*
Admiral RYDER	
Admiral FARQUHAR	. *Our great Nautical Advisers.*
Capt. DENNISTOUN, R.N.	*Surnamed Wilson.*
Capt. COLQUHOUN .	. *A beneficent Providence.*
Mr. ALBERT GREY	. *Just relieved,—only for the present, from Parliamentary duties.*
Mr. R. SHAW STEWART	. *An Ancient Mariner.*
Mr. ANTHONY TROLLOPE	. *Our Chronicler.*
Mr. CAMPBELL FINLAY	*Our Australian Authority.*
Mrs. H. BLACKBURN .	*Our Artist.*
Miss CAMPBELL of Blythswood	
Miss STUART of Montford	. *Our Leading Equestrians.*
Miss REDDIE of Wemyss Bay	
Mr. JAMES CLELAND BURNS	*Our Packer in General.*
Mr. GEORGE A. BURNS	. *Our Natural Philosopher.*

The *Mastiff* was commanded by Captain Kerr, with whom was associated

B

Captain Ritchie, a nautical authority great in ice, and peculiarly conversant with the Northern seas. With them we had a crew of thirty-two men, including engineer, seamen, stewards, and firemen ; and thus, being fifty on board, we started from just beneath the towers of Castle Wemyss on the evening of Saturday, the 22nd June, 1878. I presume it will be known to all who may read these pages that Castle Wemyss is the abode of our host, Mr. John Burns.

In the printed card of the " Mastiffs,"—a card with which every " Mastiff " was duly supplied before we started,—the names which I have given at the head of the list come nearly at the bottom, so that the four Burns' appear to be the four junior hounds of the pack ; but I, writing in my own name, have altered the arrangement, seeing that the *Mastiff* and all that was in it was the property of Mr. Burns, and that we were his guests from the moment we put our foot upon the deck till we left the vessel,—after the lapse of three weeks,—again in Wemyss Bay, under the walls of his residence. We had been summoned for Saturday, the 22nd, and were all on board the vessel that day at six P.M. A few minutes later the anchor was weighed, amidst the mingled cheers and lamentations of our friends on the shore,—lamenting, not that we were going, but that they should not have been able to accompany us.

I need hardly describe the trip down the Frith of Clyde, how we passed the Cumbraes, and Bute, and Arran, and put in on the following Sunday morning at the little harbour of Campbeltown. The beauties of the Clyde are too well known to warrant further ecstasies, even in private pages such as these. At Campbeltown we remained during the Sunday, partly in order that we might attend Divine service, and partly that we might not reach the island of St. Kilda on that day. Nowhere, even in Scotland, is a stricter reverence paid to the Sabbath than in the little western island of the Hebrides. At Campbeltown we found two services going on at the same time,—under the same roof, though a partition wall divided them,—one in Gaelic and the other in English. The majority of our party was Scotch, and no doubt they talked Gaelic quite as well as our southern language ;—but the English service had the preference.

It was considerably shorter than the other, but I do not say that that was the reason. Here, too, some of us took a long walk on shore, during which we discovered each other's political leanings,—not without a considerable amount of enthusiastic difference. Why it was that all the Scotch men and all the Scotch ladies were devoted admirers of Lord Beaconsfield, seeing that of all parts of Her Majesty's dominion Scotland is the most liberal, whereas the few anti-Scotch "Mastiffs" were quite of a different way of thinking, remained a mystery to the last. The energetic late member for South Northumberland and I,—with such poor arguments as a mere scribbler could use,—maintained the battle on that afternoon not indifferently against numbers, till the Scotch Admiral with a loud chuckle of delight, which in victorious moments seem to sound out from his features, and to be audible from every finger, told us that Disraeli is like the most important inland sea in Europe because he is the Boss for us;—(Bosphorus). Then we were cowed. The delightful riddle went home to the hearts of the ladies, and with all the truth on our side we were nowhere in the argument.

During the night we steamed away, making in the first instance for St. Kilda the farthest away, or westernmost of all the Hebrides. Here we were to call, partly because of the delight there is in seeing far away strange places, partly because the advent of such a vessel may be made a source of great delight to the poor islanders who do not see much of their brethren from the mainland, and who are, in truth, in want of such help as their brethren can bring to them. On the Monday we got into a thick fog, so that for a time we almost despaired of finding St. Kilda. As this was the only touch of bad weather we encountered during our expedition we had little ground for complaint. Nor were we very unhappy even during the fog. Those who had not met each other before became well acquainted, and there was life on board even though it seemed dull enough a few yards off. The nature of our life may be in part imagined from the drawing which our artist has made of a battle, or rather a siege, which on the afternoon was carried on with considerable energy on the deck.

B 2

The *Mastiff* is a vessel of 870 tons, 220 horse-power, lately built for the Scotch and Irish Royal Mail Service, which is in the hands of Mr. Burns and his partner, and which had thus been put to purposes of pleasure as a yacht before it was relegated for ever to the arduous duties of its future life.   On the quarter-deck, at the head of the companion-stairs, there is a little snuggery which had been fitted up as a library and boudoir, capable of containing ten or a dozen persons.   It was supposed to be Mrs. Burns's peculiar property where she might summon her ladies around her and occasionally admit the visit of a favourite virile visitor.   Such was the idea when we started on the Saturday evening; before Monday afternoon was over it was taken possession of as a smoking-room by, I regret to say, a large portion of the gentlemen, who regarded it as a convenient spot for the comfortable consumption of tobacco and whisky and water.   With this the mind of our host was so infuriated,—chiefly perhaps because he does not love tobacco and whisky himself,—that he resolved upon turning evil-doers out of the fortress.   How he failed the picture shows.   One traitor within, who was desirous of surrendering, we liberated head foremost through the window.   The others held their ground.   The thoroughly pugnacious head appearing at the window is that of an innocent and most injured indi-vidual, of a poor old gentleman who never smoked, and also very rarely partook of any strong drink.   He, however, was present on the occasion, and was there-fore bound to stick to his guns.   Mr. Burns, with a visage frightful with anger, but nevertheless as like as he can be, is attacking this gentleman with a rope's end.   Wilson,—why Wilson shall be explained before long,—is on the roof with a bucket of cold water.   Mr. James Burns with great, but quite ineffectual fury, is endeavouring to defend what should have been the sacred recess of his sister-in-law.   One of our fair equestrians is making a not altogether fair use of a tumbler of cold water.   So we were all employed when we were told that through the fog the rocks of St. Kilda had burst into sudden sight.

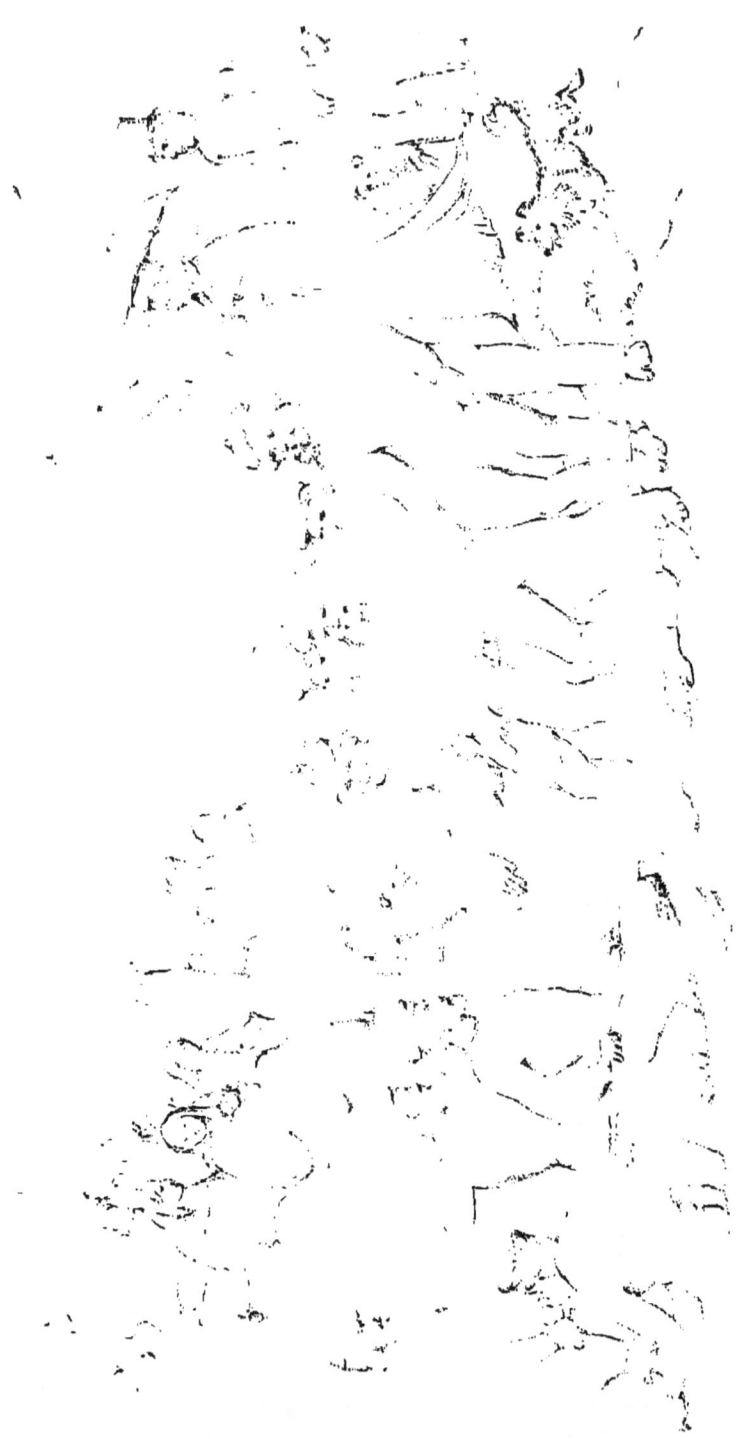

CHAPTER II

OTHING can be more picturesque than the approach to St. Kilda, seen as it was by us through the rising fog. We came upon the jutting rocks of the point suddenly, as it were, to us who were uninitiated in such matters. The captains and the mariners, no doubt, knew more about it, having felt their way gradually through the darkened water. As we glided into the little bay by which the island is approached, we saw arches in the rocks, through which the blue sea could be again seen, and the abodes of myriads of birds, which were disturbed by our steam whistle, and the sharp, serrated points of jagged cliff, all so near us that every detail was clear to our eyes. Then, by degrees, we came upon the little green valley opening down upon the shore in which the people of St. Kilda live. There were the few acres that are cultivated in the island, and there is the row of cottages, eighteen in number, in which the inhabitants live. There is also the chapel which has been built for their use, and there also lives their pastor, who has been now twelve years among them.

We went ashore in the ship's boats, and the inhabitants came out to meet us with gracious smiles. With them was their minister, and with them also was Miss MacLeod, the sister of MacLeod, the proprietor of the island,—of whose goodness in going among them and remaining with them from time to time it is impossible to speak in terms of too high praise. Charity can hardly go beyond this, seeing that every hour of her presence is to them a blessing, and that every hour of her presence there must be to her an exile.

The first care was to land certain stores,--tea, sugar, and such like,--which Mr. Burns had brought as a present to the people. It is the necessity of their position that such aid should be essential almost to their existence. Then we walked up among the cottages, buying woollen stockings and sea-birds' eggs, such being the commodities they had for sale. Some coarse cloth we found there also, made on the island from the wool grown there, of which some among us bought sufficient for a coat, waistcoat, or petticoat, as the case may be.

They are a comely, good-looking people, bearing no outward signs of want. So much I am bound to say on their behalf. But their general condition is such as to have made me at least lament that so small an island, so far removed from the comforts of the mainland, should have become the abode of a few families. It is about forty-five miles from the nearest of the large inhabited islands,--forty-five miles, that is, from humanity; but St. Kilda is in itself so small that there is no ready mode for traversing that distance. There is no communication by steamer, except such a chance coming as that of ours. The whole wealth of the small community cannot command more than a small rowing-boat or two. When we landed, the men were in sore distress for a few fathoms of rope, which they obtained from the liberality of Mr. Burns. It was thus apparent that they were excluded from the world, as so many Robinson Crusoes ; and though the life of a Robinson Crusoe, or a few Robinson Crusoes, may be very picturesque, humanity will always desire to restore a Robinson Crusoe back to the community of the world.

The island is about two-and-a-half miles long, and about seven in circumference; the highest land is about 1,200 feet high. As I have stated before, it contains about thirty acres of cultivated land, lying just in front of the cottages, on which potatoes and oats are grown. But it appeared, even in regard to this land, that it cannot return more than three to one for the seed committed to the earth. Within the memory of some of the inhabitants the returns were nearly treble what they are now. When the labour is counted up, the value of the land, and the difficulty of carrying seed to such a place,--the produce of the place itself deteriorating too quickly for purposes of procreation,—it becomes a question whether any such cultivation can become remunerative. There is, too, a considerable amount of pasture-land among the rocks and hills, on which are maintained about fifty cattle and 400 sheep; but with them there is much difficulty. The winter here is very cold, and in winter the stock is necessarily left to shift for themselves. If there are to be inhabitants in St. Kilda it is of course well that they should have mutton, wool, and milk; but still there arises the question whether the industry and attention needed for the care of the sheep and oxen might not be expended elsewhere more profitably, and with greater advantage to the persons concerned. In their want of other fuel, the inhabitants skin the turf from their pastures and burn it. Gradually, thus, the grass is going, for it is burned much quicker than it is produced. In this way the food for the sheep and cattle will quickly disappear.

Of the cottages it must be acknowledged that they are much better in outward appearance than many which are to be seen on the mainland, either in the Highlands or in Ireland, or even, I may add, than in parts of England. They are soundly built of stone, and each contains two well-sized rooms; but it may, I think, be taken for granted that this is due to private munificence and not to the personal efforts of the inhabitants. There are still to be seen the wretched hovels in which the people dwelt before the stone cottages were erected, fifteen years ago. The interior of these habitations could hardly be called clean; but could it be expected that they should be so? Cleanliness is one of those advantages of civilization which come from the frequent communication of men with men. Robinson Crusoe could hardly have been particular about his bed; and though in fiction many comforts have been attributed to him, the thoughtful reader, reading between the lines, will have recognised his many deficiencies. Those cottages, which I suspect to have been the result of private munificence, by which I mean that they have been built at an expense of money for which no adequate return was expected when they were built, are rented indeed at £2 per annum each; but the rent so paid includes the use of the cultivated land. In addition to this, 9d. a year is paid for a sheep's grazing, and some adjusted annual stipend,—I heard, but I forget what,—for a cow or an ox. But I heard also that the whole rental of the island is about £80 per annum, much more than which, if the things could be put at their proper value, is given back in charity.

The pastor, whose life here is certainly not to be envied, and who acts as schoolmaster as well as minister, receives £80 per annum from the Scotch Free Church. That also is to be counted among the charities bestowed upon the island, and is bestowed at the cost of great necessary deterioration in the energy and intellectual capacity of the clergyman selected for the purpose. That it should be otherwise is impossible. There is but one person in the island, but himself, a married woman, who can speak a word of English. No books can reach him; hardly a newspaper. To him can come none of that light which we all receive from intellectual conversation. Surely £80 on the mainland would go much farther, both for the good of the minister and for that of those receiving his ministration. We were told that some former MacLeod had bought the island for some round sum,—and as I have seen £3,000 mentioned in a published work as that given, I may repeat the figures. In return for this, he has upon his shoulders and on those of his sister, the onerous task of sustaining by his private means the existence of the community and of relieving their wants. As for the £80, we may say that it goes a very short way in reimbursing him. It is good to find a man who will do this, but it is not good to have a state of things in which such doing is necessary.

There are between seventy and eighty inhabitants on the island, of whom, among the adults, the female outnumber the male by nearly two to one. This, of course, comes from the fact that the young men can leave the harshness of such a life much more easily than the young women. I was told that at the present moment there were two marriageable young men at St. Kilda, and twelve marriageable, but unmarried, females. Nothing can be more detrimental to a community than such a state of things, unless it be the constant inter-marrying of near relations, which must be the result of a few families living together in seclusion from the world at large As far as I could learn, there were six family names among the eighteen families resident at St. Kilda. The names were as follows:—McDonald, McCrimmen, McKinnon, McQueen, Gillies, and Ferguson.

I found that they could all read, and were plentifully supplied with bibles in Gaelic. That they are a very religious people there can be no doubt,—though probably in some things their religion may run towards superstition, as must be the case in so small a community. I have said that outwardly they appeared to be a healthy and a comely race. In mechanical things they certainly are clever, making very many things for themselves which the economical division of labour throws into the hands of a few in large cities. Each man is his own shoemaker and tailor. They dye their own wool. Whatever furniture they use they make generally for themselves. They make their own candles. But perhaps the chief employment of the men is the catching of sea birds; the feathers of which they sell, and on the flesh of which they in a great part live. The bird which they eat is the fulmar. What might be the nature of its flesh to one uninitiated I had no means of testing during the few hours we spent upon the island. But in conversation with the English-speaking female inhabitant,—a Mrs. McDonald, who had been born in Sutherlandshire, and had spent there the early years of her life,—I learned that she had not very readily fallen into the way of eating the fulmar. A little bit of a very young bird even yet went a very long way with her. Sometimes they have bread. Sometimes they make a stew with oatmeal and fulmar,—not delicious I should think to any but a St. Kildarite; sometimes they luxuriate with corned mutton. Sometimes they have porridge. Occasionally they have been near to famine; and then they have been kept alive by presents,—by what we may call eleemosynary aid. A former visitor, giving an account of his visit, states that he found twenty carcases of cured mutton lying in a warehouse. But he goes on to say that the mutton had been brought from another island by the proprietor, and that they were his property. This transaction was no doubt comfortable to the island; but I doubt whether it redounded to the profit of the owner of the mutton.

I have said that the St. Kildarites appeared to be healthy From a medical report, however, published by the same traveller, Mr. MacDiarmid, it appears that they are greatly troubled with rheumatism and scrofula. But the curse of the island in regard to its sanitary condition is a disease among babies for which the cause has not yet been discovered. At about eight days old the children die. That this was so I heard from every side. It seemed to prevail to such an extent that a child at that age would be more likely to die than live.

Such is St. Kilda;—a most picturesque point in the ocean at which to land and at which to marvel at the beautiful freaks of nature. But it is an atom of land hardly intended by nature as a habitation for man. What spots among the broad waters should be taken in hand and made available by man for his home, and what should be left in their desolation is a question very difficult for man to answer;—but I think it may be taken as a rule that no region can be of real value, the products of which must be eked out by charity from other regions. Many a rich and useful country will not provide itself all that it wants; but no country can be rich and useful unless it can provide itself by supplying its own wants, or can purchase what it requires by the sale of its own products. This certainly is not the case with St. Kilda.

After wandering among the cottages for an hour or two, and making acquaintance with the people, we swarmed down upon the beach, all the inhabitants accompanying us. Among them were Miss MacLeod and the minister, who already seemed to be almost old friends. The men helped us along the slippery rocks, and took us by the hand over and over again. Many of them went on board, not unnaturally desiring to satisfy some little want, and to see the last of their strange visitors. There was that coil of rope that was so much desired by the whole island;—and the English-speaking lady had lately been unwell and desired a little brandy for her stomach's sake. As far as I could learn there was not a drop of spirits upon the island, so that some of the worse evils of the larger world had been escaped by the inhabitants of St. Kilda. I had made that lady's malady my peculiar care, and I handed the brandy to the lady's husband. Then we steamed away, I think, amidst their blessings, certainly amidst their cheers.

Who shall say that these people ought to be deported from their homes and placed recklessly upon some point of the mainland? I have not the courage so to say. They themselves, if they were consulted, would probably be averse to such deportation. Were they so deported each individually would suffer, at any rate for a time, by the change. We

> " Rather bear those ills we have
> Than fly to others that we know not of."

But yet their existence cannot be good for them, and certainly not for their posterity;—and as far as we can judge a time will come when that posterity must die out unless the people be removed. In the meantime it appeared to me that all is done for them that present kindness can do. And so the "Mastiffs," having seen all that there was to be seen at St. Kilda, went on upon their adventurous voyage.

CHAPTER III

HE Faroe Islands was the destination to which the "Mastiffs" were next bound. I doubt whether much is at present known about the Faroe Islands in the polite circles of British society. That a great deal may be learned about them by inquiry is, no doubt, true; but then so few people do make inquiry about the Faroe Islands! There are seventeen of them, some of which, however, are uninhabited. They belong to Denmark, and lie nearly half-way between the Shetland Islands and Iceland. Strömö is the chief, and of Strömö, and of the Faroes generally, Thorshavn is the capital. At Thorshavn we landed on the night of Tuesday, 25th June.

I must here remark that we had already proceeded beyond the regions of night,—beyond the regions of night, that is, in this period of the year. In midwinter there are but seven hours of daylight at Thorshavn; but that deficiency is made up to the inhabitants by the possession of twenty-four hours of light in June. We were in Thorshavn for three hours, from about 10.30 P.M. to 1.30 A.M.; but we found all the people up, and were accompanied by a considerable portion of the population as we made our little tour about the town and neighbourhood.

When our boats landed us,—which they did very conveniently on a rock, but, as we were assured, not at the grand landing-place,—we were met by a gentleman in uniform, who addressed us in excellent English. The language of the people is a dialect of the old Norse, but that of the court, churches, and schools is the modern Danish. This gentleman, however, as did some others

who escorted us, spoke English also. He told us that he was the postmaster. I doubt whether there are many postmasters in Great Britain who could address a Faroeite stranger in his own tongue, or even in Danish. The postmaster of the Faroe Islands was in face singularly like Mr. Gladstone, and therefore may be endowed with some of that linguacious capability for which Mr. Gladstone is so renowned. The *Mastiff* had, of course, been sighted for some time, and as, even at Thorshavn, steam vessels such as the *Mastiff* do not come and go daily, a crowd had come down to welcome us, with the postmaster at its head.

The entrance among the islands had been very lovely, the bold headlands of one after another shewing themselves in rapid and quick succession. None of our mariners, well-provided as we were with mariners, had been there before, and therefore they were forced to recognise the promontories and bays simply from the chart; and, as time was an object, and as our general speed was about twelve-and-a-half knots an hour, a good deal of sharp looking-out and of deduction was necessary to enable us to go straight into the roadstead of Thorshavn without fault or delay. But by dint of consultation among the mariners, and by what I call deduction, – that headland must be that headland because that bay must be that bay, and that island that island,—we accomplished the work, and did not beat about looking for a port, as must have been done in the ancient days when Captain Cook felt his way about among strange shores. Was he, in truth, such an awful-looking personage as he appeared to be on the wooden pedestal which was erected for some time amidst the clubs in Pall Mall!

The postmaster, with a considerable proportion of the population, was there, on the rocks, to receive us. I wonder whether they would have been snug in bed had the *Mastiff* not hove into sight, or whether any of them had gone to bed, and been extracted from their slumbers by the tidings of our approach ! I did venture to ask a question on the subject of a kind-hearted English-speaking Faroeite, who soon attached himself to our *cortège;* but it seemed to me that he took a pride in making believe that a Faroeite, having twenty-four hours of daylight, never thought of bed. He remarked that, as it was broad daylight, the

people were of course walking about.   I should imagine, however, that they went
to bed after we left them.

We were taken first to the postmaster's house,—only, I think, because the
doing so was an act of hospitality.   Here we found ourselves in a very pretty
room, comfortably furnished, overlooking a beautifully picturesque nook of the
sea.   I myself, the present Chronicler of the " Mastiffs," have served among
post-offices, and have had much to do with postmasters.   I should have liked
to have asked this gentleman what was his salary, and what his duties, and
whether there ever came an inspector from the head office in Denmark to look
after him.   I fancy that he must have been more than postmaster,—that he
probably holds high office among the Governor's advisers, as with us our noble
Postmaster-General, Lord John Manners, has a seat in the Queen's Cabinet.
He would hardly have had so very pretty a house had he been only postmaster,
nor so imposing a uniform.

We were told that the Governor was in bed.   He was the only person in the
island as to whom such a fact was acknowledged.   But though he was in bed, our
host thought that duty required him to pay his respects in person.   He therefore
had the Governor extracted from his bed, and paid his respects.   The Governor,
with but one eye open, but still with much graciousness, expressed the delight he
had in welcoming the " Mastiffs " among the islands.

Then we proceeded upon a walk, a number of men and a long string of pretty
maidens accompanying us.   We went about among the narrow streets,—streets
which are required for no wheeled vehicles,—and saw other maidens looking at
us from out of the windows.   These streets were not rectangular, straight, and
ugly, but ran crookedly here and there, up and down hills, round the little indented
bays of the sea, with houses standing sometimes angularly, sometimes with gables
to the roadway.   And the houses were all covered with green turf, with turf that
at this time of the year was growing,—a mode of roofing which gave a singularly
picturesque appearance to the place.

The turf is used as a protection against snow, and is a protection of which the " Mastiffs " saw more when they found themselves in Iceland. That it should have been found necessary here I am surprised, as Thorshavn though it lies between 61 and 62 N.L., is not a place of very much snow. The climate is moist and foggy, and storms are frequent; but the winters are not severe. The frost lasts hardly beyond a month, and the harbours are seldom icebound. But there are the houses covered with grass, giving to the place from a little distance the appearance of a town under the sods.

When we had perambulated the streets we were taken up to a little hill over the town so that we might look down upon and see the nature of its situation and its structure. Thorshavn lies all around various little nooks of the sea, and has that smell and flavour of the sea which is peculiar to such places. It is very pretty, but its smell and flavour, combining that of many fishes, is one to which the visitor must become accustomed before it will be palatable. There is certainly the ancient and the fish-like smell;—otherwise Thorshavn is delightful.

There are, I was told, about 10,000 inhabitants in the islands, of which the capital holds about 900. Looking at statistics composed as to the Faroes about twenty-five years ago, I find the number of the people given as 8,150 for the group altogether, and 1,500 for the capital. The figures which I have given are what I received simply in conversation. The population of the town was probably correctly stated by my informant. The cultivation is very poor, the ground being too rocky for the general use of ploughs. Horses and cattle are rare. The wealth of the farmers consists in their sheep. The sheep, however, are never housed, and the wool is torn from their backs instead of being shorn. Here, as at St. Kilda, there is a great enterprise of bird-catching, for the sake of the flesh as well as the feathers. There seemed to be little or no poverty. A good carpenter in Thorshavn would earn 4s. a week; in other parts of the islands a moderate carpenter would earn 2s. They use Danish coins, of which the crown contains 100 farthings; this crown is worth something over 2s. The people generally are healthy; the girls appear to be remarkably strong. But here again I was told that rheumatism prevails.

When we descended from the hill we were carried to other parts of the town,—especially to see the church. It was now considerably past midnight, and yet there seemed to be no difficulty in finding the key. The church was spacious,—not at all unlike one of our own ugly churches, with pews, and a gallery, and an organ. It seemed to me to be larger than would be wanted in England for a population of 900; but it is probably the case that a larger proportion of the population attends Divine service than is the case with ourselves. It was evident that they were proud of their church, and that they who accompanied us were anxious that we should see it.

Some of the shops were open,—whether for our special benefit, or because it is the custom of the Faroeites to carry on their trade at midnight, we did not know. But cigars were bought there, not made I believe of the very best Havana tobacco, and sugar plums. One of our ladies, Miss Stuart, at about one o'clock in the morning, having observed, examined, and admired the shoes which the young ladies of the island wore, expressed a wish to purchase a pair. She was immediately supplied from some ready-made shoe warehouse. But as the concomitant long red strings with which the Faroe ladies tie them up their legs were wanting, and as the shoes were imperfect without them, one of the girls immediately stripped off her red strings and presented them to our young " Mastiff." I hope she may wear them for many years in honour of her far away friend in Thorshavn.

When the affair of the shoes had been transacted, we were summoned on board by J. B. It may be as well understood by all readers that J. B. is the name by which our host has been known, I was going to say familiarly, but I may add generally, in all social, fashionable, and nautical circles. J. B., with the mariners, had made their calculations as to reaching Reykjavik, the capital of Iceland, at a certain hour, and would allow us no further time. A little we were delayed by parting embraces in the postmaster's house, and by the desire which the presence of a post-office not unnaturally created in the bosoms of some of us to write letters to our friends from so remote a shore. The letters were written, and I am told actually reached their destinations,--which I think says very much for the postmaster himself and for the Danish Government generally.

Then we went on board, and to bed. As I drank my little drop of whisky and water before retiring I could not help feeling how strange it was to have seen an entirely new country since tea-time. Had I lived for two years in the capital, I might perhaps have known the people better and have had a clearer idea as to their habits of life. But it really seemed to all of us that we knew the Faroe Islands better than we should have done by reading all the books that could have been written about them.

CHAPTER IV.

REYKJAVIK.

E coasted along the southern and south-western shore of Iceland, wondering at the vast expanses of frozen snow which filled the slanting valleys down almost to the shore, with various opinions. Were they glaciers, or were they only fields of frozen snow? There was a regular battle of the glaciers, fought with many field-glasses and telescopes. I own that I took the part of the simple snow, thinking that the colour to be seen in glaciers was absent. But I must own that the evidence went against me. They were of immense size, perhaps a dozen miles broad and thirty or forty long.

Very early in the morning we found ourselves in the harbour of Reykjavik, the capital of the country, and as we looked out upon the waters of the fiord in which we lay, and saw the islands and headlands around us, every "Mastiff" felt that he or she had done something memorable. The first operation of the "Mastiffs" of the sterner sex was to bathe, which was done with the greatest satisfaction from the ship's ladder. The water was deliciously tranquil, deliciously warm, deliciously cool,—beautifully pellucid as sea water can only be when it is altogether tranquil. The bathing was so charming that the bosoms of the ladies were filled with envy, and before long they had a boat put off for themselves, so that they might find some spot of perfect oceanic seclusion. They declared to us afterwards that they were in all respects successful.

After breakfast we swarmed ashore, impatient to touch the land of Iceland. We were all of us desired in the first instance to present ourselves to the Governor. J. B.'s orders in this respect being of a nature to admit of no denian, I think that we all went thither in a string, except our friend Denniston, upon whose generous mind had settled down a whole world of vague fears, lest some "Mastiff" might by chance come to sorrow during our journey. Hence was he soon christened Wilson by the "Mastiffs" in general, whose minds were not unnaturally filled at the moment with Lord Dufferin's book. As Wilson was to that modern a prophet of evil, so was our friend to us. But of all the miseries which he predicted not one occurred, and we all believed him to have been Christian enough to rejoice at the non-completion of his own vaticinations. Cassandra I have no doubt wished the evil things to come to pass as she foreboded them :—and so, probably, did the original Wilson. But our Wilson was of a better heart than his namesake, or than Cassandra.

Governor Finsen, the Governor-General of Iceland, received us all, swarming as we did into the drawing-room, with the greatest cordiality. Mrs. Finsen soon joined him, with others of the family, and seemed to think it quite natural that sixteen English ladies and gentlemen of whom she had never heard before, should be sitting on her chairs and sofas. Would a governor of ours in the West Indies have welcomed sixteen miscellaneous Danes as cordially? All the information required by us was at once given, and we were put upon the proper track for finding a guide and a stud of ponies for our purposed ride up to the Geysers. We found the Governor living in a comfortable wooden house, with many rooms opening from one to another on the ground floor, with a large drawing-room looking out on what would have been the garden at the back of the house, but that gardens in Iceland are not easily maintained. Some flowers and vegetables in front of the house we did see,—and I observed a frame for protecting plants from frost; but it soon struck us that the absence of the growth of pretty things was one of the chief drawbacks to the comfort of life in Iceland. There is not a tree in the island :—not a wild grown shrub. A small cabbage is a difficult achievement.

From the Governor's house some of us went to that of the Bishop's. J. B. had

it all cut and dry in his own mind, having quite settled with himself what the
courtesies of life demanded from a pack of "Mastiffs" arriving suddenly in the
capital of a new country. All presented themselves before the Majesty of the
Civil Law. It was essential only that some few of the elders should recognise the dignity of the Established Church. But at the Bishop's we became
acquainted with Thora, the Bishop's daughter. Thora, before we left, had
become to all of us the heroine of Reykjavik. Even Wilson, the unhappy one,
was softened altogether by the charm and wit of Thora, and became quite devoted
and almost gay in her presence.

Having thus performed our duties we were allowed to roam about the town,
and as we had ladies with us we very soon found ourselves in the jewellers'
shops,—for Reykjavik has jewellers' shops. Old silver ornaments, silvered
belts and filigree work, all of which had probably come some years ago from
Denmark, and some of which had possibly come from Birmingham, was there
for sale,—and were sold. Each "Mastiff" wanted some token to take home to
England, and the tokens were for the most part taken home in the shape of
these ornaments. And we were frequent at the shop of a certain saddler who
sold leather sachels and whips for riding. Every "Mastiff," male and female,
required a whip and a sachel,—for had it not been appointed for us that we
were to ride up to the Geysers; and how could we ride unknown ponies unless
armed with whips, and how could we endure to be separated from our baggage,
as must be the case, unless provided with some means of carrying our most
needed little treasures? We emptied the shop of whips and sachels, and left
the saddler, I should hope, happy in his mind.

Reykjavik, as Thorshavn, is a fishy town. Along the unoccupied parts of
the street, or the shore, at every little bit of vantage ground which could be
found vacant, there were fishes laid out to dry; and it seemed that every
portion of the fish was preserved with care, including the bones and head and
jaws. It is interesting to see how the wants of a people will accommodate
themselves to the products which nature is able to give to them. Bread is very

scarce in Iceland; but it would almost seem that dried fish would do as well. It seems that their mutton is very good,—so good as to be declared by the Governor to be equal if not superior to any produced elsewhere; but it is not plentiful, and therefore of course dear. It is very generally salted,—as must of course be necessary for winter consumption in a country in which the winter lasts for more than six months, and in which the stock must be kept alive during the period by fodder provided for them.

I do not think that any one of our party ate a morsel of Icelandic food during our sojourn beyond curds, cream, and milk,—unless it might be a biscuit taken with a glass of wine. Our provisions had all been brought from Scotland, and from our ship's stores we carried with us up to the Geysers what was needed. The " Mastiffs " therefore are not in a position to say much from their own experience of Icelandic delicacies or Icelandic nutriment. But the look of the people, which is better evidence than personal trials, declare the viands to be generally wholesome. They are a healthy, comely race to the eye, though of course they have their own sanitary troubles, as do other people. Scurvy, cutaneous diseases, and even leprosy are to be found; but then, so in other countries are consumption, and heart disease. Considering the sparseness of the population, and the difficulty as to medical advice which must be incidental to such a state of things, they are a healthy strong race in spite of their want of cereal foods. It was whispered into my ear that drunkenness is not uncommon. I saw no one drunk, nor do I think that any case of intoxication was seen by any " Mastiff " during our sojourn. Lord Dufferin speaks of a high state of conviviality on a certain occasion; but, if I remember rightly, it was his own conviviality which has been chiefly described. The " Mastiffs " themselves, though jovial dogs, were nevertheless sober dogs.

The real condition of a people, as to happiness and civilization, may very generally be told from the state of education among them. Everybody, almost everybody, in Iceland can read. I quote as follows from Sir George Mackenzie's work on the country, published as long ago as 1811, when educa-

tion was much less rife in the world at large than it is now;—" By the super-
intendence of the priests and the long-established habits of the people, a regular
system of domestic education is obtained." . . . " The instruction of his children "
—that is, the ordinary Icelander,—" forms one of his stated occupations; and
while the earthen hut which he inhabits is almost buried by the snows of winter,
and darkness and desolation are spread universally around, the light of an oil
lamp illumines the page from which he reads to his family the lessons of knowledge, religion, and virtue." He goes on to say that by an old law of the land
the clergy are empowered to prevent a marriage when the betrothed female is
unable to read. The strictness of this latter rule we in England would not be
prepared to recommend; but the feeling, the desire for and practice of education
from which it emanates, tells us of a condition of things which even yet we ought
to envy in parts of Great Britain. The amount of reading which certainly does
prevail throughout Iceland is marvellous. There is hardly in the island what can
be called an upper class. There is no rich body, as there is with us, for whose
special advantage luxurious schools and aristocratic universities can be maintained. But there is a thoroughly good college at Reykjavik, with a rector and
professors, at which a sound classical education is given; and there are now also
minor schools. The result is to be seen in the general intelligence of the people.
" Macbeth " has been translated into Icelandic, and published at Reykjavik,
which would not have been done unless there had been some one there to read
" Macbeth." There are five newspapers published in the island, two of them at
Reykjavik. J. B. caused some hymns to be printed at a day's notice, in order
that they might be sung during Divine service on board the *Mastiff*. The work
was excellently done.

The one deficiency in Reykjavik which the most surprised me was the want of
a bank. There is no such thing as a commercial bank in Iceland. The population of the island was stated to me to be 90,000, and of the town to be 2,500.
The latter probably was overstated; but there is a body of intelligent well-
educated men and women quite sufficient, one would have said, to demand the

convenience of a bank. The imports and exports are considerable, fish, oil, skins, tallow, and wool being sent away in exchange for timber, wood, tea, sugar, and all those thousand little articles of comfort which a civilized community uses every day almost without knowing it. But nothing can be imported or exported without payment being rendered in the old world fashion of barter. The man who brings in so much wood, or so much tea, must take out so much wool, or so much fish. We promise to pay, such as we use when we circulate bank notes or bills of exchange, is unknown, because there is no bank. The visitor going to Iceland must provide himself with coined money sufficient for all his wants. The Queen's head on an English sovereign seemed to be very popular with the people at large.

Reykjavik, as a town, is at present clean and pleasing. It consists chiefly of two parallel streets, with small cross streets, and a small square in which there is a statue of Thorwalsden, and at the corner of which stands the large Lutheran church, containing a font given by Thorwalsden, with bas-reliefs on the sides of the pedestal by himself. The sculptor's father was an Icelander, and the sculptor himself is therefore the great hero of Iceland. The church itself is anything but beautiful, but is large and commodious.

In a solitary walk which I took round by the back of the town, where lies a little lake with marshy land around it, I found a number of women and children turning the peat for drying, or sending away in baskets on their ponies that which was fit, carrying on their operations very much as they do in Ireland. Fuel to them is a matter of great solicitude. During eight months of the year artificial warmth is necessary; and not only have they no coals, but neither have they wood. Coal imported from Scotland may be bought at Reykjavik; but as there is no carriage for anything through the country except on the backs of ponies, very little coal can ever be seen beyond the limits of the town.

CHAPTER V

HILE we were all engaged in the frivolous pursuits of buying silver ornaments and talking to the good-natured people in the shops,—all of whom seemed to possess a little English,—J. B., intent upon graver matters, was asking all the greater people of the town to come and eat a dinner on board the *Mastiff*. This was done on a Friday, and the dinner was to be eaten on the following Saturday. It was necessary to crowd a good deal into a little space, and J. B. was determined that every "Mastiff" should do his or her duty. A kinder host I never knew, but have seldom served a sterner lord. Now it was considered proper that, in addition to the dinner, we should have a picnic on one of the islands. There was no other day for the picnic but that which was to be utilized also for the dinner. The "Mastiffs" went through them both manfully, and I do not know that a dog among us was the worse for it. With what superhuman efforts the cook got through the work in hand, it was not my province to enquire. The food as it was wanted appeared. I must mention in this place,—so that the marvel in regard to the cook may be duly enhanced,—that we all intended to start on the Monday morning on our route to the Geysers, carrying with us over a hundredweight of cooked meat and the bread necessary for our journey.

On the picnic Thora the divine accompanied us. All languages seemed to her indifferent. Of English at any rate she was mistress. We sailed in the ship's boats over three or four miles of water, and were landed on an island especially devoted to the breeding of eider ducks. From the eider ducks comes the eiderdown of which are made those stuffy, fluffy, soft, slippery coverings which always fall off a German bed when an Englishman tries to sleep in it. I do not at all like eiderdown myself, but it might be very well to have an eider duck farm in Iceland, with 2,500 ducks, and feathers at 12s. a pound.

We were at first taken up by Thora to the proprietor's house, where we immediately went to work and bought all the silver ornaments. The Icelanders were, without exception, very nice, but they seemed to like English gold. Why the ornaments were there, displayed before us on a large piano, I could not understand. But there they were, and we bought them instantly. The house seemed to be an excellent, large, old-fashioned grange, round which there were many farm outbuildings. At the back of the house was the drying-ground for the eider feathers, which seemed to be the main produce of the estate.

The whole island belonged to the proprietor, who welcomed us at the house, and he took us out to show us his birds. One we found seated on her nest, made of her own feathers. The maternal victim plucks the down from her breast and makes her intended nursery. Then the down is taken away, and she does it again. A second time the robbery is committed, and she makes a third nest. Beyond that she will not go. If pillaged again she abandons her intentions in despair. The third nest is therefore left, and the young birds are reared. But when she has taken out her young ones, there is a third crop to be garnered, as good as ever.

Our lunch was spread for us in a most picturesque spot, at which we were joined by the proprietor and his son, a young boy, who had delighted us by his knowledge and skill as to the birds. It was here that Thora made herself so divine that our Wilson seemed altogether to succumb to her attractions. Will he or will he not return to Iceland? Should he do so, and should he succeed, no doubt he will go into orders,—that being the fitting condition for the son-in-law of a bishop. If so we cannot doubt but that he will rise to high ecclesiastical distinction in the island.

We hurried back from our lunch that we might prepare ourselves for the grand dinner. I may perhaps be supposed to have thrown some slur upon Iceland food in what I said in the last chapter, in which I have acknowledged that bread and fresh meat are scarce with them. But no one can say a word against Iceland appetites. When we sat down to dinner at half-past seven we had altogether forgotten that stupendous lunch on the grass.

The dinner on board the *Mastiff* was an affair which certainly will not be forgotten by any of us. Of ourselves there were sixteen. We were always sixteen, and never were separated, except on one occasion, which shall be mentioned in the next chapter, when a little grace was allowed to a lady on account of extreme fatigue. Together with these sixteen "Mastiffs" there feasted the fourteen distinguished Icelandic guests whose names I will add in order that a full record of the banquet may duly descend to posterity. They were as follows:—

Governor HILMAR FINSEN, and his wife, Lady OLUFA FINSEN.
Mr. THORBERG (*Governor Prefect or Amtman*) and his wife.
Mr. A. THORSTEINSON (*Treasurer*).
Bishop P. PJETURSSON, and his wife.
Miss THORA PJETURSSON, his daughter (*our particular friend*).
Mr. J. PJETURSSON (*Head of the Superior Court*).
Mr. J. THORKELSON (*Rector of the Latin College*).
Mr. J. ARNASEN (*Inspector of the Latin College*).
SIGRIDUR JONSDOTTER and GUDRUN KNUTSEN (*two beautiful young ladies in full Icelandic costume*).
Mr. JON JONSSON (*Sheriff of Reykjavik*).

Thus we made a party of thirty, and considering that the banquet was given on the shores of Iceland in the harbour of Reykjavik, we thought that it was very well done. The portrait of the *Mastiff*, duly dressed with flags, as she received her distinguished guests on board while her guns were being fired, may be seen in the accompanying photograph. I trust that the smoke of the guns may be duly observed. J. B. was particular as to the proper firing of the proper number of guns and nearly blew us all into the water. The *Mastiff's* boats in which the distinguished guests arrived cannot be seen because,—well because they were out of sight, on the other side of the vessel.

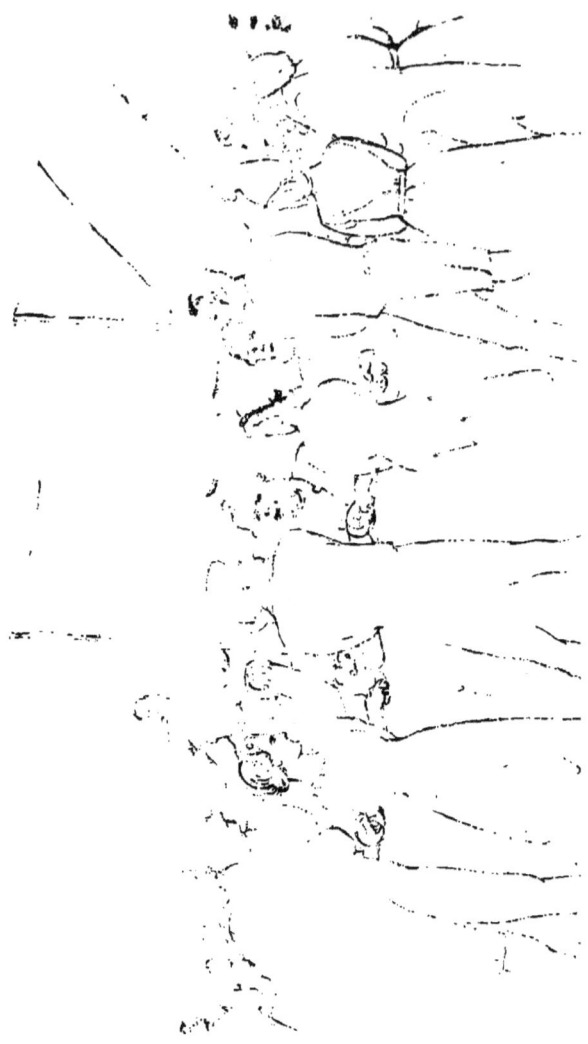

It was my privilege, being older than the other "Mastiffs," to sit on the left hand of the Governor's wife and to have Thora next me on the other side. Never was a man so happily placed! Thora, however, being by this time quite an old friend,—almost a " Mastiff,"—and having as an old friend to amuse others around her, I devoted myself chiefly to the Governor's wife. She also spoke English, and was thus enabled to tell me much of her family, much of her life, and much generally of the ways of life in the country. I have been acquainted with many an English lady for ten, twenty,—for thirty years, without knowing so much about her, as I did of the Lady Olufa Finsen. She was a comely, brown, pleasant, smiling lady, with a large face, bright eyes, and a look of homely good-humour that I have never seen excelled,—a lady certainly to be remembered. And she had much to say about her children, the education of her boys in Copenhagen, and the comforts and discomforts of her Icelandic life. She herself and her husband had come from Denmark;—but she was quite willing to be at home at Reykjavik. The Governor himself spoke French; most of the others English. There were one or two less fortunate who when excluded from the use of their own languages, Danish and Icelandic, could express themselves only in Latin. In Latin conversation I do not think that any of us " Mastiffs " made much way.

After dinner we had three toasts proposed to us by J. B. The first was of course in honour of our own Queen. The next, equally of course, was drank to the honour of the father of our own dear princess, the King of Denmark, within whose territories we were sitting. The next was to the honour of our guest, the Governor. He responded to us in French, bidding us all a hearty welcome to Reykjavik and wishing us success in the little trip we were about to make up to the Geysers. Then we had the ladies' health, and after that we went up on the deck for a dance.

It was now about ten o'clock, and it was of course broad daylight. I have often been present at dances given on board ship at night-time,—commonly in the tropics when the air has been sultry, but when it has been necessary that lamps should be hung about the rigging so that the ladies might see where to place their feet. Here no lamps were necessary, but the chill air made it expedient that we should all keep moving. The effect of the continuation of day upon those not used to it is very singular. One is not reminded to go to bed, and so one sits and talks and roams about till there comes a feeling of fatigue which is at first hardly intelligible. Then the last cigar would be thrown away, the last drop of whisky and water would be swallowed, and we would hurry off to our daylight couches,—astonished as they say the cocks are when they are brought from England to Iceland and do not know when they ought to crow. There was no feeling of not knowing when to crow on the occasion of this ball, for it was all crowing;—but it was impossible to get over the feeling that everybody was dancing in the middle of the day.

Thora was dressed as she might have been dressed in Paris or in London. There was reason no doubt for the difference of apparel, but to us it was mysterious. Perhaps Wilson knows. Our other Iceland beauties, Sigridur and Gudrun, were there in the full picturesqueness of their native costume. It was all very unlike the dresses of our own girls; but most unlike no doubt in the head-dress. This consisted of a white hat, with, I think, yellow bands to it, made something in the shape of Minerva's helmet, with the crest turned forwards. From this depended a light veil covering the shoulders, and hanging down the back, but leaving the face free. Then there was a jaunty jacket, partly open in the centre, with large bright buttons down the front and on the sleeves. The skirt beneath was of some bright colour, projecting forward like an extinguisher, coming even quite down to the ground so as to hide the feet, but with no inclination towards a train. In fact it seemed to be of exactly the same length before and behind. The head-dress, as may be seen in the excellent portrait furnished by our artist, for which Sigridur had that morning sat, is very pretty. The costume as a whole is picturesque and the jacket is becoming;— but I am not sure but that in regard to personal grace Thora did well to adopt the habits of more southern countries. All that we might probably learn from

Wilson. It was late before the Governor and his party left us, amidst the loudest cheers which all the "Mastiffs" and all the crew could give him.

On the Sunday morning, having first had our own service on board the ship, - and having sang our hymns as printed in Reykjavik, - we went to the Reykjavik church. There we found many of the girls and not a few of the married ladies dressed in their full national costume, as Sigridur and Gudrun had appeared at the dinner. Sigridur and Gudrun were there with the same jaunty little helmets and same jackets. I fancy, however, from what I heard, that Reykjavik would not have been so decorated on that Sunday but that the British strangers were expected at the church. It was whispered that an order had been given that the beauty of Reykjavik should be seen at its best.

The service was long,--two hours and a half; and the hymns were many,-- five, I think, in number. Of the minister's sermon none of us could understand a word, but it seemed to be impressive. He was remarkable for a very stout, stiff, large white ruff round his neck, as though he had come out of a Dutch picture; and, wearing this as he walked away from the church, he seemed to be treated with most profound respect.

On our return to the ship our baggage was at once ordered from us,-- whatever any "Mastiff" required to be carried up for him to the Geysers. "Send what you want," said J. B.; "but pray don't send what you don't want." I wanted two great coats, a rug, a blanket, two or three changes of linen, a suit of clothes, a pair of boots, a pair of slippers, a brush, a toothbrush, a bit of soap, two towels, a mosquito net, and a big stick. Looking at the great mass which we carried I do not think that I was more unreasonable than others.

CHAPTER VI

"BREAKFAST at four," said J. B., as we parted on Sunday night. There was a little whispering among us that five would do very well, and that absolutely punctual obedience was not to be expected from a pack of full-grown "Mastiffs." But J. B. rendered disobedience impossible by making such a row about the ship, bodily extracting every recusant hound from his kennel at three, that by four we were almost impatient. Mr. James Burns, who, after dancing a Scotch reel for the amusement of the Icelandic beauties on the Saturday evening, had passed the remainder of the night in packing up, was found all alive at the same duty very early on Monday morning. He had, however, been punctual in the meantime at the divine services. We had our bathe off the ladder; by four we were at breakfast; and at five we were mounting our ponies on shore.

There were sixty-five ponies in all. The idea was that each "Mastiff" should have two,—one to rest the other,—that the cook and the two servants who went with us, and the five guides, should have such aid, each to his own pony, as might be necessary, and that the remainder should be laden with the provisions, tents, and baggage generally. I may here say for the advantage of future travellers in Iceland, that the ponies cost about £1 per head for the journey, including the guides. As the "Mastiffs" were forbidden to allude to money,—everything of that kind coming either direct from the clouds or from J. B.,—I perhaps am out of order in making this allusion. I did, however, hear that such was the amount paid.

It was an awful moment, that of the selection of the ponies. No " Mastiff " wished to seem to take the best ;—but no doubt every " Mastiff " wished to have the best. Before we came to the journey's end our ladies even knew very well how to mount themselves, and what each could do on each pony when they were mounted ; but at our first starting there was hesitation. As I looked at the large stud, as they stood all grouped together on an open spot near the Custom House at which we had landed, I recognised the unpleasant fact that I was the heaviest of the party,—very much the heaviest. The pony subjected to me must carry something over sixteen stones. We had almost fairy " Mastiffs " among us, under whom any pony would be delighted to gallop all day ; and among our "Mast ffs" who certainly were not fairies, there were some not much afflicted with a too solid weight of flesh.

Our head guide was one Zoega, who is I believe well known to Englishmen who have required guiding in Iceland. He was not only guide, but contractor, finding all the ponies and making the necessary arrangements for us along the roads. Our provisions, as I have stated before, were our own,—or rather J. B.'s. One of our admirals, Admiral Ryder, with a skill that was truly admirable, made minute calculations as to the amount required of each article. I have no doubt that after this he will always be selected by the First Lord to provision her Majesty's entire fleet,—so adroit was he and so sufficient. If it be so the sailors will be no doubt as well satisfied as were the " Mastiffs." As to myself I raised an humble word only in regard to the liquor, gently advising J. B. not to be too profuse ! He was profuse ;—but not one of the pack,—not even one of the attendant pack,—was in the least the worse for it.

It became Zoega's duty to apportion the ponies. At the first starting no one liked to make a personal request. And most among us probably felt that a bad selection made by the rider himself could not be made matter of complaint,— whereas a bad beast allotted to one might be made matter of severe comment. With true solicitude at my heart I allowed Zoega to mount me as he would,—and I believe that he gave me not only the worst pony in Iceland, but the most

pernicious brute that ever was foaled in any country that ever possessed mares!
O Zoega, why did you so treat me? The animal no doubt was strong;—would
have carried Daniel Lambert had he been willing to carry anything. Perhaps
after all it was a compliment. Perhaps Zoega thought that no other man there
was hero enough to ride such a brute! I did make him carry me the first half
day's journey,—some eighteen miles. His plan was to linger behind persistently,
and then, when the others were all out of sight, to turn round and make his way
back to Reykjavik! I had almost expended all the strength left to me in thrashing
him, when at last he owned himself vanquished and went slowly forward. After
that I think no one rode him. I declared that nothing should induce me to put
my legs across him again. From that time out, however, the animals supplied to
me were wonderfully good.

I have made many journeys on horseback in the course of my many travels,
continuing them sometimes for many days together, and certainly of all those
that I have made this was done at the quickest average pace. I have generally
found five miles an hour all through to be as much as would get itself accomplished. Here we made nearly seven. As the party was large of course there
was much straggling, and the van would reach its resting place long before the
rear. If there was a fault as to our too great pace, it rested altogether with three
young ladies, who among the " Mastiffs " always led the way, driving on before
them an, I must say, not unwilling young guide. Trotting was our usual pace,
but trotting did not suffice for our fair equestrians. In the East and the West, in
Syria and Central America, I have found it expected that I should never get out
of a wretched amble, unless it was to fall back into a walk. In Iceland I was
often going at a very fair pace for fox hounds.

After a ride of four hours,—which was at any rate four hours to me,—we
rested by a river side for our luncheon. Every one was supposed to have brought
his own luncheon in his own wallet. Then it was that that noble hound, Colquhoun, came forth, not indeed for the first time but in the strangest manner, as a
specially ordained beneficent Providence. Out of one waistcoat pocket came a

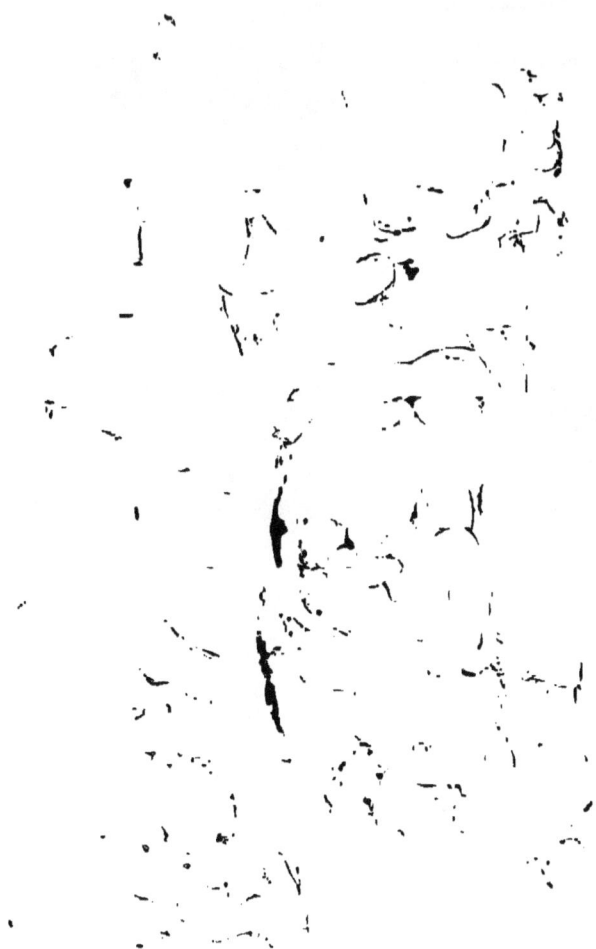

large round kettle,—out of the other a spirit lamp, a bottle of spirits, tea, sugar,
and a tin of preserved milk. In five minutes the fairies among the "Mastiffs"
had all been served;—in five minutes more all even who were not fairies had
lapped their cup of tea. These articles, the reader will say, might have been
carried on the spare ponies! With such a cavalcade why require a Providence
with such waistcoat pockets? The reader knows nothing about it. The cavalcade
with the provisions had gone on the night before,—or, otherwise, we should have
had no dinner on arriving at Thingvalla. We never got to our rest together with
our pack-horses; but we cared the less about that because Providence with the
tea-kettle, tea, and spirit lamp was always there.

Our second journey for the same day was on to Thingvalla,—Thingvalla, with
the astonished traveller, as described by Lord Dufferin. It must be supposed that
all into whose hands these pages may fall will have read of Thingvalla and the
astonished traveller. To me the second ride was delightful because I had done
my punishment, and was carried along pleasantly in the front on an excellent little
steed. But yet when I got off my pony on the spot on which the astonished
traveller is seen seated on his, I was very stiff. All were tired enough, though
there was a courage about the ladies which forbade them to complain and a
spirit about the men which forbade them to seem weaker than the ladies.

Thingvalla is a wonderful place, very picturesque, worthy, in itself, of a journey.
Taken as a whole it was perhaps of all that we saw in Iceland the most worth
seeing. Down from the spot on the brink of the cleft in the rock at which the
traveller arrives so suddenly, there is a steep descent through an almost precipitous
rift in the cliffs to the broad green valley below. It has all been formed by
volcanic action. The broad valley, perhaps eight miles broad, has been made
by volcanic force. About, through and across the valley, are deep narrow
perpendicular rifts in the rock, made of course by the same agency. And yet
nothing can be greener than the valley, seen, as it was by us, in June. On
descending we had to wade through what seemed to be two or three rivers. Here
we came to a parish church,—with which we afterwards became very intimately

acquainted, and with the minister's house of which some of us knew the details very well before we left the place.

In the churchyard our tents were pitched and dinner laid. While we were preparing for dinner news which at first seemed to be very sad was told of one of the party. Mrs. Burns, our hostess, could not go any farther. The pony selected for her had been uncomfortable, and the heat and labour of the ride had been too much for her. J. B. and the minister had already discussed the matter, and she was to remain as guest with the minister's wife. This she did, J. B. remaining with her, till our Providence had galloped on to the Geysers, seen them, and then returned; so as to liberate J. B. from his attendance. When this was done J. B. also galloped on to the Geysers, and came back with the rest of the party. In this way Providence and J. B. had a good deal to do,—which they did like " Mastiffs."

About a quarter of a mile from the church, at the back of it, with a delicious walk to the place among the rift-divided meadows, is the Althing. The Althing is a spot among the pasture lands on which used to assemble the Parliament of the Icelandic Republic. That such meetings were held there cannot, I think, be doubted; but the Parliament was, probably, rather judicial than legislative. Decisions of the Supreme Court were given before a frequent assembly by the wise ones seated on a rock. That is the idea which, thinking about the Althing of Thingvalla, I have formed in my own mind. The spot consists of a narrow field perhaps 400 yards long, and, though very irregular, fifty broad on an average. But to it there is but one possible mode of entrance, by a narrow gangway through the deep rifts in the rocks. Along each side, meeting together in a point at the top, there are these rifts, perhaps thirty feet deep, the sides of which are perfectly perpendicular, and at the bottom of which there is dark, black, deep water, most mysterious, almost infernal to be looked upon. Our Artist made a wonderfully correct sketch of the place, which the reader will see. On the right hand were the abrupt rocks of the ravine down which we had come, with a waterfall tumbling over them into the rivers; away in the front, beyond the

church, was the beautiful expanse of the Thingvalla lake; and around on every side the exuberantly rich grasses of the meadows. Within the Althing itself the wild flowers were most exuberant.

During the night the ladies slept in the church and the men in the tents. Some serious observations were made as to nocturnal noises,—particularly as to one special sinner. But it never was quite decided among us who was the sinner. The ladies who were shut up in the church at a distance declared that they had been much disturbed. They had their own opinion;—but never mind! When we sat down to breakfast at five o'clock in the morning no blood had been shed.

Our ride to the Geysers was again divided into two stages, each nearly twenty miles,—supposed to take four hours each, but which the leaders did in something less than three. The drawback to our comfort on this day, we knew, would be that as our baggage ponies would travel much slower than ourselves, we should have no dinner and no tents ready when we got to the Geysers. That we should have to wait was impressed upon us;—and with this was the impression that tea would not be instantly forthcoming because our Providence would be otherwise occupied. But we took with us, each his lunch, and perhaps a little drop of whisky. I observed at least that some others did so. The Ancient Mariner was often kind to me in offering the use of his flask. At our resting-place on this day huge bowls of milk, washing-basins full of milk, were brought down to us from a neighbouring farm-house.

A few miles on from thence we came to the river Brüará, crossing it at a spot so beautiful and so singular that it will always rest on my memory distinct from all other river scenes. Here again Mrs. Blackburn drew a very correct sketch of the place, which will explain its nature. A delightfully rapid broad and clear river comes rippling down from the mountains close at hand; the body of this, however, is so shallow that there is no difficulty in riding a pony across it; and from the nature of the bottom the ford would be as good as the road,—but that in the very centre of the channel there is a narrow rift, perhaps twenty feet deep, into which the waters boil and bubble, so that the opposing waterfalls nearly meet each other with their crests. And this rift must be traversed by the traveller. For this purpose there is a little wooden bridge fixed on each side on the rocks beneath the water, riding over which the equestrian seems to have but very little protection between himself and the defile into which the waters are pouring beneath him. The ponies, however, knew the spot, and where a pony would go, any " Mastiff," male or female, will ride him. About 300 yards below the ford there is a high rock jutting out into the river, from which is to be had perhaps as pretty a river scene as ever I saw in all my travels.

Some miles beyond the Brüará it was benevolently suggested by the elder Zoega that he would gallop on to a certain farm about three miles off and, as our own provisions were in the rear, have provided for us such comforts as the farmer could supply. Then it was that a passion for fast riding first came upon our ladies. Zoega started in a gallop, and,—truth compels me to state the fact,—Miss Stuart would go with him. There fell upon Zoega a strong desire to reach that farm-house alone,—but an equally strong desire on Miss Stuart to be there with him. When Zoega got off his pony at the gate, Miss Stuart, at the same moment, slipped off from hers at the same spot. A gallant " Mastiff" or two endeavoured to keep them company, and our Ancient Mariner did make the running very good ; but the pace was too great, and the young lady only was there to see Zoega dismount. After that, till we were back at Reykjavik, there can be no saying which of the three young ladies rode the hardest. Miss Reddie at last got an ugly lanky pony which for a while enabled her to leave every one in the lurch. Miss Campbell would for awhile take up the running so that we were inclined to back a little red wall-eyed animal which she rode against the field. But the passion had come upon them ; and though J. B. strove masterfully and loudly, and though Zoega strove with anxious looks and bated voice, from that hour forth there was no stopping the pace till we had again reached Reykjavik. " There was racing and chasing on Cannobie Lea." " What are we to do for a doctor if they break their necks ? " said J. B. almost sobbing in despair. It was of no use ! As a cautious elder, I spoke a word. I was simply whistling to the winds while the riders were already rushing away far in front.

As one result of the fast riding we got our coffee at the farm-house, called Muli, and had also an ample opportunity of seeing the appurtenances of a comfortable Iceland grange. Our meal consisted chiefly of curds, cream, and sugar, which some of us pronounced to be excellent, and of which some of us ate very heartily. The curds were a little sour,—but were so deluged with thick cream that I thought them to be delicious. The coffee was not perhaps so good. The farmer's wife was delighted to allow us to wander about the place, into the bed-rooms, kitchen, parlours, larder, and dairy. The parlour in which we sat was comfortable, and for a farm-house, well furnished. I will not say that the beds were inviting; but that was not to be expected. In one room there were four stout bedsteads, each with its feather-bed. The kitchen was roomy, dark, and mysterious. Perhaps the most interesting apartment was the dairy, with its numerous arrangements for milk and cream and cheese. The larder also was a good sized room and stored amply with provisions; but the contents of the larder were not so appetizing to an Englishman as those of the dairy. Altogether there was an appearance of great plenty about the place. The house was built, as had also been that of the minister's at Thingvalla, with various gables all looking one way, with grass on the roof, and the roof coming almost to the ground. The construction is arranged altogether in reference to snow, so that the snow itself should afford protection against the cold, and then run off without causing damp. Round the grange there were rich wide pastures, with beautiful grass. At another farm a little distance I saw some wire-fencing about the place, showing how far agricultural civilization had progressed even in Iceland.

After remaining at Muli nearly two hours, we galloped on, and soon reached the field of the Geysers which was about four miles distant.

CHAPTER VII

ERE we were at the Geysers! To most of us, I think, the Geysers had been the chief point of attraction. As I had seen the Geysers of New Zealand, and had learned how inferior were those in Iceland, I cannot say that it had been so to me. But the Geysers even of Iceland are a sight to see, and I was glad to have an opportunity of visiting them. Our ride to and from the Geysers, with Thingvalla, the Brüarä, and our galloping "Mastiffs," will always be dearer to me than the Geysers themselves.

We reached the blasted field,—the field blasted by continual eruptions of hot boiling water,—about six; and as our baggage ponies were still far behind us we had ample time to roam about and explore the not distant wonders of the place. The hot springs in this locality are probably all within a mile of each other, and the two Geysers,—as the intermittent fountains of boiling water are called,— perform their operations within a quarter of a mile of each other. Between the two our tents were at last pitched, so that we might be close at hand to see whatever was to be seen. As we walked about we went very carefully among the boiling holes, as a single false step might precipitate a foot into one of the small infernal subterranean kettles. In an hour we had seen nearly all that was to be seen. Then the tents came, and we bivouaced and dined among the springs. There was of course no darkness or even twilight, and we had now abandoned the idea of dividing the twenty-four hours into day and night. So we wandered about, dabbling in hot water, and anxiously looking for eruptions.

There is, first of all, the Great Geyser. This consists of a pool of boiling

water about fifty yards in circumference, two or three feet deep, in the midst of which there is a round funnel about eight feet broad, descending, as far as the eye can judge, into the very bowels of the earth; up this the boiling water is emitted. There is always a supply coming, for a certain amount of hot water is always running out on the two opposite sides of the pool. Here the " Mastiffs " amused themselves by dabbling with naked feet, scalding their toes when they went too near the pool, warming them comfortably at an increased distance. Excavations suitable for bathers there are none,—as there are so delightfully formed and so deliciously filled at the Geysers in New Zealand. At a little distance, in a ravine, there was a hole in which some of us endeavoured to sit and wash ourselves. Occasionally, perhaps once in every four hours, a large and violent supply of hot water is thrown up the funnel of the Great Geyser which has the effect of disturbing the basin and ejecting the hot water from it rapidly. This occurs with a noise, and is the indication given of a real eruption, when a real eruption is about to take place; but the indication too frequently comes without the eruption. This, when it does take place, consists of a fountain of boiling water thrown to the height of sixty, eighty, some have said 200 feet. During the twenty-four hours that we remained at the place there was no such eruption,— no fountain, although the noise was made and the basin was emptied four or five times.

About a furlong off from Geyser Primus, which is called the Great Geyser, is Geyser Secundus, to which has been given the name of Strokr,—or Stroker, as I may perhaps write it. Stroker is an ugly ill-conditioned, but still obedient Geyser. It has no basin of boiling water, but simply a funnel such as the other, about seven feet in diameter, at the edge of which the traveller can stand and look down into a cauldron boiling below. It is a muddy filthy cauldron, whereas the waters of the Great Geyser are pellucid and blue. This lesser Geyser will make eruptions when duly provoked by the supply of a certain amount of aliment. The custom is to drag to its edge about a cart load of turf and dirt, and then to shove it all in at one dose. Whether Stroker likes or dislikes the process of feeding is left in doubt. He bubbles about furiously with the food down in his gullet for half an hour, and then rejects it all passionately, throwing the half-digested morsels sixty feet into the air with copious torrents of boiling muddy water.

These are the two Great Geysers. Around are an infinite number of small hot springs, so frequent, and many of them so small, that it would be easy for an incautious stranger to step into them. All the ground sounds under one's feet, seeming to be honey-combed and hollow, so that a heavy foot might not improbably go through. Some of these little springs are as clear as crystal. In some the appearance is of thick red chocolate, where red earth has been drawn into the vortex of the water. Sometimes there is a little springing fountain, rising a few inches or a foot. Had there been no other Geysers, no other little lakes of boiling water known in the world, those in Iceland would be very wonderful. When they were first visited and described such was perhaps the case. Since that the Geysers in New Zealand have become known ; and now the Icelandic Geysers, —if a " Mastiff" may be allowed to use a slang phrase,—are only second-class Geysers.

What time we went to bed I do not remember. As we intended to remain at the Geysers all the next day, waiting for eruptions if they would come, and then to start on our back journey in the evening, we were not very particular as to hours. At some early morning hour, when we were in bed, J. B. arrived, having been riding all the night, and riding all the night in the rain. In Iceland they say it generally rains when it does not snow. This night's bad weather was all that we had. What we should have done, had it been wet, with our tents, or, worse again, sometimes without our tents, with ladies wet through, with every-thing foul, draggled, and dirty, no " Mastiff" can guess. Luckily not a drop fell except during those early morning hours through which poor J. B. was on his solitary ride.

On the next day there was more dabbling among the hot springs, and the ladies essayed to wash their stockings and handkerchiefs, thinking it good fun to have their boiling water provided ready for them by nature. Miss Campbell,

however, was heard to remark that should it be her fate to follow out the profes-
sion of a washerwoman during the remainder of her life, she would prefer to be
supplied with an ordinary washing-tub and stool.

Such were the Geysers. The spot itself is wanting in beauty or prettiness,
because the subterranean heat and the continued eruptions destroy the growth of
grass, and give a weird, blackened, ill-omened look to the place. There is a hill
on one side, and that also seems to have been blasted, and on the other a river
into which the waters from the springs make their way. But the river is defiled
with sulphur. The place is curious, no doubt, but not beautiful. Of the Geysers
themselves our Artist has done the best in her power to give the reader an idea
clearer than the writer has conveyed.

Then came two days of galloping home, or rather two nights, for we rode
chiefly during the night. Cannobie Lea was nothing to it. When Miss Reddie
could get a-head with her lanky brute, there was nothing for it but to gallop after,
regardless of danger. But on our return journey an additional impediment was in
the way. J. B.—prudently remembering the absence of the too probably to be
needed surgeon, instigated perhaps by Zoega mindful of his ponies,—made strong,
I may say violent, efforts to stop any young lady in her attempts to forge a-head
upon the road. Often he succeeded. But it did occur more than once that the
combined equestrian forces would be too many for him. On the return to Thingvalla, which was made in a very hurried fashion, he succeeded cruelly in barring
the way of Miss Reddie. I never felt more inclined to fight for an injured
damsel. But as he did so Miss Stuart went by him like a flash of lightning, and
disappeared headlong down the road in front.

We reached Thingvalla about three in the morning, hot with riding, cold
with the waters of the rivers through which we had ridden, and very tired. We
had carried some supper and eaten it on the way, and had had bowls of milk
brought to us. Now we should have been altogether provisionless, had not our
Providence been there with his tea-kettle. It was arranged that we should all
sleep in the church. The tents and baggage were far behind us, and we were

G

very tired. A certain amount of exclusiveness, however, was still allowed to the
ladies even in this arrangement. They slept upon the steps round the communion
table, and were walled off by a little ecclesiastical rail. The men slept two and two,
down the nave, or little passage rather, which ran down between the seats. Here,
again, our Artist has done much more than I can do to describe the scene. Some
of our party reposed in the gallery, and one irreverent hound insisted on ringing
the church bell during the night. There was a rumour that this was done by our
Artist herself, who had crept up to the place in order that she might exercise her
art, and portray us as we were lying;—but I have reason to believe that this was a
calumny. The night was passed with many noises. No sense of the solemn
nature of the place, or of the near vicinity of the ladies, sufficed to repress some
exuberant hounds who seemed to be unused to the proprieties of kennel life.
During a pause in the growling, when all had just lain down, a voice in silvery
tones proceeded from the direction of the communion rail:—"Mr. Speaker, I spy
strangers in the gallery!" The Ancient Mariner declared that he was tickled;
—but he need not, therefore, have disturbed all Thingvalla with his roars. This
was so bad at one time that an elderly "Mastiff" got up and made a speech,
—"Would not the 'Mastiffs' remember that there were ladies there,—ladies
who were very tired,—ladies who would certainly wish to sleep?" Then there
was heard a gentle suppressed titter which seemed to come from some locality
near the communion table. I had expected to find the minister indignant on
the following morning, because of the desecration of his church; but the minister
took it in good part, bell-ringing and all. What passed between J. B. and the
minister nobody knew. I imagine that there was a pleasant moment. At any
rate we parted from the family amidst expressions of devoted friendship.

It was again in the evening that we started on our last day's ride, and I own
that I left Thingvalla with soft regrets, as I told myself that I should never again
see that interesting spot. Thrice I had bathed in its rivers, and had roamed
about it till I seemed to know all its nooks. It is a place full of nooks, because
of those wonderful rifts,—and full of greenness. I had not cared much for the

Z... ., The Gnoo

Mr. Campbell Finlay.

Mr. Albert Grey.

Miss Campbell (Blythswood

Admiral Farquhar.

Mr. J. Cleland Burns.

Admiral Ryder.

Mrs. John Burns.

Mr. John Burns.

Miss Stuart (Montford .

Mr. G. A. Burns.

Mr. Anthony Trollope.

Miss Bloof.

Captain Colquhoun.

Mrs. Hugh Blackburn.

Mr. Robert Shaw Stewart.

Captain Dennistoun, R.N.

Geysers, but Thingvalla and the Brúara had been very charming to me. It was strange to me that there should be a place in Iceland so beautiful and so soft as Thingvalla with its lake.

One little incident must be told to the honour of Admiral Farquhar, than whom no "Mastiff" could possibly be more gallant. The Admiral is a great fisherman,—and there were two other fishermen both great, our future Northumbrian Member of Parliament, and our Australian "Mastiff." They had heard much of a certain river, running out of the lake many miles away, so filled with fishes that nothing of the like is known among all the waters best loved by fishermen. But——! Our friends were told that there was a drawback. The fishes were not to be doubted;—but neither were the flies! Zoëga believed that no Briton could stand there, even for the catching of a single fish.

So instigated, our fishermen were determined to try. Were they not provided with mosquito nets? It may as well be mentioned here that there is not such a thing as a mosquito in Iceland. Our fishermen went forth in happy spirits. "Flies!" said the Admiral with scorn as he arranged a salmon rod about as big as a bedpost; and prepared himself in his impenetrable breeches, in his boots and his huge covering net. They left us at a point on the road, aware that they were about to add eight hours of additional riding to their already heavy work. But for such fishing as that what will not a fisherman endure? They went. They caught a fish;—one among them. And then they were driven,--not ignominiously indeed,—but, ah, too certainly from their ground. In five minutes they became fly-enveloped, so as to be able neither to do, nor to see, nor to speak. The one fish was flung to the ground, and they escaped from the fatal field as fast as their ponies could carry them. There is a picture of our Admiral as he caught that fish,—a marvellous portrait. But I fear that it is in private hands and cannot be obtained for the use and delight of our readers.

As we rode back to Reykjavik we had our tents pitched, and slept for three hours on the way. Then, at six in the morning, we streamed into the little town, and were at once photographed on our ponies as we sat. There, O reader, is the pack, there are hounds and there are the horses! Some of the likenesses are very good, especially that of our fisherman, the Admiral, and of J. B. and his wife. Our young Naturalist, George Burns, is said to have behaved badly as he sat, thinking no doubt of his birds and eggs. He cannot be congratulated on the likeness. But when it is considered that we had to wake up a photographer at six o'clock in the morning at Reykjavik, to photograph us all at five minutes' notice, I think it will be acknowledged that the group is very well done.

CHAPTER VIII.

" Parting is such sweet sorrow,
That I shall say goodbye till it be morrow "

T was thus that every "Mastiff" felt as we made our rapid way back from Reykjavik to Wemyss Bay. We had done thoroughly what we had intended, and to get home was all that was left to us as "Mastiffs." But there was a melancholy in this which perhaps would have been less had we not been so happy together.

We returned by a different route, passing down between the Hebrides and the coast of Sutherlandshire, but not touching at any point till we landed Miss Campbell at Balmacara opposite to Skye. Thus for many hours we steamed along the magnificent coasts of Western Scotland, beginning with the Butt of Lewis on one side and Cape Wrath on the other, looking into Gairloch and Apple-cross as we passed, and running through that most lovely of all sea channels, the narrows between Skye and the mainland. Here we left Miss Campbell at the wave-washed door of a friendly house, whence two young ladies came to greet us on the rock on which we landed her. It would be difficult to find a more romantic spot. It was between ten and eleven, but it was still daylight and the colours of the woods and the waters were as perfectly beautiful as colour can be imagined, when I shook hands with our fair friend as I left her. It was sad to part after having been so intimately thrown together for a time !

We had heard no news for three weeks, and when we landed at Balmacara, J. B. and I, with Miss Campbell under our charge,—we did not know whether we were or were not at war. Then we learned that the affairs at Berlin had straightened themselves, that the Russian had been smoothed and the Turk protected,—and that the Englishman who had lately bristled with so many arms was to be regarded as a peacemaker by the world at large.

We passed on through the Sound of Mull and during the night left Mrs. Blackburn at Oban on the shores of Argyleshire. By Jura and Isla we steamed on, and round the Mull of Cantire, and up, north again by Arran and Bute. Thus having surveyed the whole west coast of Scotland,—we made our way up the Frith of Clyde, and anchored in Wemyss Bay about three o'clock on Monday, July the 8th, having been just sixteen days on our journey. Back from Reykjavik the distance by the route we had travelled is 911 knots, and we had travelled this at the rate of thirteen knots an hour. Here the pack of " Mastiffs " was split up separately into separate hounds, each hurrying away to his or her home. There was a little eating of cream and strawberries at Castle Wemyss, a little attempt at ordinary shore courtesies, a returning as it were to the dull ways of life on shore. But we all felt that this was to be done painfully, each by himself in solitude. And so with many pressings of the hand, but with few spoken words, we left our host and hostess and went away in melancholy humour to our own abodes.

www.ingramcontent.com/pod-product-compliance
Lightning Source LLC
Chambersburg PA
CBHW020314090426
42735CB00009B/1341